STORIES
F O R
B O Y S

**BOBCAT
BOOKS**

LONDON/NEW YORK/SYDNEY/COLOGNE

Edited by Mike Teasdale

Book Designed by Alison Goodhew

ISBN 0.7119.1111.8
Order No. BOB 10054

Exclusive distributors:
BOOK SALES LIMITED
8/9 Frith Street, London W1V 5TZ, UK.

MUSIC SALES CORPORATION
24 East 22nd Street, New York,
NY 10010, USA.

OMNIBUS PRESS
GPO Box 3304, Sydney,
NSW 2001, Australia.

To the Music Trade only:
MUSIC SALES LIMITED
8/9 Frith Street, London W1V 5TZ, UK.

Photo credits: Joe Bangay (4/5, 13, 32),
Santo Basone (39),
Adrian Boot (8, 18, 23),
Mike Cameron/Rex Features (45),
Chicago Peace Museum (39),
Andre Csillag (2/3, 52t),
Leslie Fratkin (10, 22, 34, 47),
London Features International (56, 58, 59, 60),
Barry Plummer (11, 16, 46, 52b, 61),
Rex Features (25),
Paul Slattery (14, 17, 20, 26, 28/9, 30, 42, 43),
Syndication International (40),
Kees Tabak/Rex Features (1, 36, 37, 51, 52m),
Debra Trebitz (48).

Typeset by Qwerty, London and
Capital Setters, London.

Printed by Commercial Colour Press,
Forest Gate, London.

ACKNOWLEDGEMENTS

I was not able to talk to U2 during the course of my research for this book, but that is not to say that they don't have their fair share in what is, after all, their story. In order to facilitate this, I have kept journalistic interference to a minimum, preferring simply to document the rise of U2 through the eyes of an observer, logging facts and illuminating them with the band's own remarks and comments and, of course, opinions.

I would, therefore, like to thank the following publications for the use of quotes and additional information: Melody Maker, Zig-Zag, Record Collector, New Musical Express, Record Mirror, Music Week, Rolling Stone, Billboard and Sounds. Also, Lynden Barber, Adam Sweeting, Paolo Hewitt and Gavin Martin, whose own interviews with U2 have proved especially helpful; the British Institute for Recorded Sound, for the use of their invaluable archive collections; Peter Doggett and Michael Cox, for their assistance in compiling the discography, and Jo-Ann Greene, for unstinting help and inspiration above and beyond the call of duty.

Dave Thomas, 1987

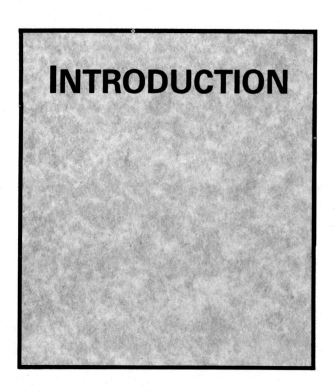

INTRODUCTION

There have been few success stories quite as pure and simple as that of U2. They arrived in London in November, 1979, four wide-eyed Dublin teenagers, bemused and bewildered by life in a city a million miles removed from that of their home town. In Ireland they were already superstars; in England they were totally unknown. Nine people turned up to see them when they made their British debut.

Today London is old hat, a short hop across the Irish Sea, just another stop on world tours which see U2 packing out venues across four continents. In Europe, no festival billing is complete without them. In Australia, they have attracted some of the biggest audiences that country has ever seen. In America, U2 spearhead a "British" invasion the likes of which have not been seen for two decades. They are, as *Big In Japan* points out, a lot bigger than most of the bands who return from Tokyo with tales of mass hysteria and buckets of yen. Today, U2 are a phenomenon.

Yet when they started, it would have been hard to imagine a more unfashionable band. The anger and aggression of the punk era had long gone, and guitars were regarded as some stubborn anachronism, long since superseded by the joys of computers and synthesizers. The New Romantic movement was approaching its peak and even the traditional haunts of rock'n'roll, places like the Bridgehouse in Canning Town, were giving their stage over to the new breed of musician who didn't need to sweat for months over a book of chords. U2 represented a return to the old values, their four piece line up the most conventional in rock. But they also represented a whole new approach to those most hackneyed of ideals, their playing and writing packed a punch which, once word had got around, was to quite literally change the whole face of modern music.

And word did get around. Once they'd got a bit of muscle behind them, once their gigs actually got advertised instead of being tucked away in the bottom left hand corner of last week's gig guide, once people started to see them, that was when the word started to spread. Quietly at first, a whisper here, a mutter there. A live review, unstinting in its praise. Then another, than another. If there was a hype, at least it was an honest one. The people who came out and said U2 were the most exciting thing they'd seen since way back when were speaking from the heart. They meant it. And people believed them. Within six months, U2 had put the damp cellars and grubby clubs far behind them and were striking out on their first headlining tour of Britain. They returned to Dublin not legendary but at least well known. The next time around they were even bigger. And the next time, and the time after that. By the end of 1984 not a dozen venues in Britain could hold them.

It isn't only their concerts, either, that have taken them this far. Album by album, U2 have grown, moving from the unconscious adrenalin of *Boy*, through the watershed of *War* and on to the sophistication of *The Joshua Tree*. When that album came out, early in 1987, Bono joked that it was named after a pile of prickles. Listening to it, letting it get inside you, it felt like a pile of prickles too, niggling barbs which simply worked themselves deeper the more you tried to dislodge them. "Smart people," he said, "put on the album and think to themselves 'I'm gonna play this a lot of times.' Foolish people would put it on and just go WOW! YEAH! and think they've got a line on it." Judging by the amount of time *The Joshua Tree* went on to stay in the charts there would seem to be an awful lot of smart people out there, listening to U2.

Nine years on – what has kept them together? "Fear of our manager," responds Bono. And how do they rate themselves musically? Bono reckons he's only now actually developing into a real vocalist, and claims, "Edge doesn't know a lot of the chords he plays. He makes them up." And what about their so-called social conscience? A lot of people have been suspicious of that although only a fool would need to *listen* for a moment to know that theirs is an intensity that could not be faked. "In school I read about the Nazis and Dachau and I thought this was some warped era the world had gone through and that it was all over now. For me to find out ten years later that there's more torture and dismemberment of human beings right now than there ever was at the peak of Nazi Germany is enough to make me want to do something about it," said Bono. The sleeve of *The Joshua Tree* gives three addresses for Amnesty International.

"People think the reasons I'm attracted to Martin Luther King or Gandhi or Jesus Christ is that in some way I'm a real man of God myself. In truth the real reason I'm attracted to these peaceful men is I'm the guy with the broken bottle. I grew up that way and I despise violence, I despise the violence in *me*, and that is why I'm attracted to men who've turned their back on it." He admits that for many people, U2 are as real today as those same men of peace were in their day. He admits also that as icons go, he's not a particularly good one. "The reason that I'm attracted to a man like Martin Luther King who could turn the other cheek is because I *can't* turn the other cheek. I'm the very person who'll nut the guy next to me, I'm the very person who in a rage will do . . . the things I don't want to do." Basically, he adds, "People mistake the music for the musician."

But do they? Simply by confessing his own failings Bono has proved himself a man of honesty, and while The Edge can tell the group's fans that "I don't see it as *our* music, we don't own the notes or the words, we've been given a gift of musical talent and this is the net result," the popularity of U2, the music *and* the musicians, is derived first and foremost from that honesty. It is this honesty which has kept U2 from stagnation. Their music is always questing, always searching. A line from *The Joshua Tree* probably sums them up best: I have climbed the highest mountains, I have run through the fields . . . but I still haven't found what I'm looking for."

Adam Clayton

CHAPTER ONE
IN WITH A SHOUT

U2 formed towards the end of 1977 at the Mount Temple school in Dublin. It was the era of punk rock, an explosion of raw musical aggression which, in the wake of the Sex Pistols, The Damned and The Clash, spread throughout the British Isles. In Wales, The Table were doing the standing still, in Scotland, Johnny And The Self Abusers sang of dead vandals and The Rezillos' baby did good sculptures, while across the Irish Sea in Belfast, bands like The Undertones, Protex and Stiff Little Fingers took the first steps towards defining a local sound which could cut across all sectarian barriers and unite the youth of that troubled city in a way that the politicians and peacemakers never had.

From Dublin, The Radiators From Space made the first impact on a national level. They were an early New Wave signing to the Chiswick label and, despite accusations of a self depreciating compliance to 'sub-Clash English punk', their *Television Screen* was an impressive debut which deservedly became a near permanent fixture in the alternative charts. But it was another six months before Dublin truly burst on to the rock and roll map. In September 1977, The Boomtown Rats followed up a well received tour supporting Tom Petty with their debut single, *Looking After Number One*. Backed up by an impressive marketing campaign which included everything from daubed slogans (Rats Eat Heartbreakers For Lunch) on the walls, to the offer of a cardboard rat arm band on the single sleeve, *Looking After Number One* reached Number Eleven in the British chart. Two months later, their eponymous debut album made the Top Twenty and, within just eighteen months, The Boomtown Rats were possibly the most important band in the country. Their *I Don't Like Mondays* became one of the highest selling UK singles of all time.

It was into this atmosphere of energy, conviction and determination that U2 were born. Adam Clayton, an ex-Public school boy serving out the remainder of his school life at Mount Temple, was already a member of a local group, a rebel and a misfit even in a school which prided itself on its unconventionality. The establishment was very much an experiment; the teachers, in the words of one of Adam's contemporaries, '...were different. They were very open.'

According to Larry Mullen the school was ...the first comprehensive in Ireland. Girls and fellahs and it was non-denominational, so there was a real effort made by the teachers for the students.

'What they emphasised was that if people were interested in something in particular, say someone was good at sport, they would push that person at sport to really help them, rather than discourage them because it wasn't academic.

'And that's what happened with the band.

Larry Mullen

We were all interested in music, and worked hard at it, so teachers came behind us and really started to push and work us. They gave us a room at school to practise in, a really good room, and one teacher in particular, the history teacher, was really helpful and he took the responsibility for it.'

In the days before the band got off the ground, though, Adam Clayton '...stuck out like a sore thumb. He used to drink coffee in class and the teachers just got used to it. He got accepted as being really quirky. He wore a kilt.'

It was Larry who was the motivating force behind U2 forming. One afternoon, he pinned a message to the school notice board, calling for potential musicians to join him in a group. Adam, of course, applied immediately. So did Paul 'Bono' Hewson and Dave 'The Edge' Evans.

'It was a combination of four individuals who, apart from the band, were totally different as personalities,' Bono explained later. 'The Edge picked up guitar — I played at that stage as well. Larry was good on drums.' And Adam? 'Adam had the only amplifier so we never argued with him. We thought this guy must be a musician, he knows what he's talking about. He used words like "gig", "action" and "fret". Then we discovered he wasn't even playing the right notes! He couldn't play at all!'

Although the four band members all knew each other by sight if not by name, comparative age differences meant Larry immediately took something of a back seat in the band — a role which, even today, he still relishes. When U2 are interviewed, Larry can usually be found as far away from the action as he can get. He is the youngest member of the band and so would have had little cause to associate with Bono, The Edge and Adam at school, had the band not come into being. Bono claims his first memory of Larry comes from '...when we were first starting off. We were at our first rehearsal in his kitchen and all these girls, all these fourteen, fifteen year old girls, kept climbing over the walls and looking in the window at Larry. Larry just shouted at them and told them to go away. And then he turned the hoses on them! He's not interested. Larry likes to play drums.'

The group's earliest repertoire consisted of cover versions, the transition to writing their own material coming with the realisation that, try as they might, they simply could not play other people's songs. 'The ideas came before the music,' says The Edge. 'We were together and it just sort of evolved into music. But at that stage it was just amusement. It wasn't anything particularly serious, although we all had deep interests.'

Bono, in particular, could see the band as little more than a way of killing time during free periods at school. Chucked out of University for not speaking his native language (Gaelic), Bono's chief interest in life was playing chess. For him, pop music had been summed up one Thursday evening in June, 1971: 'I was watching Top Of The Pops and saw Middle Of The Road singing *Chirpy Chirpy Cheep Cheep* (a particularly loathesome nursery rhyme which outsold everything in sight that summer). I must have been about eleven at the time and I thought "Wow! This is what pop music is all about. You just sing like that and you get paid for it!"'

When questioned about other influences, Bono will remark simply: 'The Who *Live At Leeds* was a very important record in my life.'

U2 played their first concert at the school early in 1978. According to Bono, it was '...one of the greatest we've ever played. It was another two years before we played another one like it. Even from the start we wanted something like the power of The Who and something that was as sensitive as Neil Young, how on edge he can be. We always wanted that. (But) our main influences in the group are each other. They're not outside. The most powerful music is created naturally, is not forced at all. It just comes out.'

As time went by, the band found themselves more and more in demand on the Dublin pub circuit, despite the fact that neither the group or their audience were actually old enough to be on the premises. On one memorable occasion, the group played a gig in a car park, simply so their fans could see them.

Early in 1979, U2 entered the *Guinness And Harp* talent contest. It was done mainly as a joke, U2 arriving at the venue straight from '...this thing called Paddy's Punk Party.' Bono had lost his voice, and he admits that 'we were a shambles, especially against all these professionals and heavy rock bands. But I knew we had something. I knew the effect we had over the audience, compared to the other bands with all their tight music and pompous playing. We made use of the fact that we were slightly fragile, (just like) when we recorded our first demos in a four track studio and couldn't get a big sound out of it. We had to work on the fragile sound. We built this

Dave 'The Edge' Evans

band around a spark. We could only play three chords when we started, but we knew there was an excitement within just the four people and even when playing to ten people we seemed to communicate that. Even though we were technically lacking at that stage, we had a spark.'

The spark had become a blaze by the time U2 played at the *Guinness* competition. They won easily, surprising nobody but, perhaps, themselves, and were offered a recording contract by the Irish wing of CBS. A three track single duly followed, entitled *U2:3*. It was co-produced by the band and former Sounds journalist, Chas de Whalley. *Out Of Control* was the lead track and it was very aptly titled. With a speed that could never have been anticipated, the single shot to the top of the Irish chart. The follow up, *Another Day*, was just as popular, while an appearance on a Dublin compilation, *Just For Kicks*, alongside eleven other local bands, did much to excite interest in the United Kingdom. And finally, U2 swept the board when the Dublin based Hot Press paper conducted its annual readers' poll. They topped five different categories. It was time for U2 to start broadening their horizons.

In December '79, U2 made their first trip to London. They played a handful of gigs, spread over a fortnight; amongst them was an evening at the Hope And Anchor, a pub in Islington, where the band attracted just nine paying customers! The following night, they opened for the all-girl group, The Dolly Mixtures, at the Rock Garden in Covent Garden. The gig was covered by Melody Maker, but the reviewer, Mark Williams, gave not a word to the support band. For that gig, incidentally, U2 appeared in Melody Makers' gig guide as V2. Six days later, at the Canning Town Bridgehouse, they were billed as UR.

Paul McGuiness, the Dublin business man who had become U2's manager around the time they signed to CBS, set up another short season of English dates for the band in March. It was to be a far better publicised trip than before and, in the light of their domestic success, hopes were high. Yet the outing seemed doomed from the outset. The evening before the band were due to leave for England, their publisher withdrew half of the promised advance money. The band arrived in London unsure whether they would even be able to survive, and there was talk of simply taking the first record company offer to come their way, merely in order to live.

12

PAUL «BONO» HEWSON

Their fears were unfounded. With only a couple of gigs under their belt, U2 found English audiences just as receptive to their brand of high energy music as any in Eire. Reactions such as Paolo Hewitt's July '80 Melody Maker review were almost common-place. He described U2's performance at the Hammersmith Clarendon as '...easily the finest display of awe-inspiring rock that I've witnessed in a long time. It contained just about every emotion that rock attempted to evoke — from anger to savagery, beauty and that indefinable essence where words become useless...'

'The first time I came to London I was really ...not shocked, but the biggest impression I had was that of the sexuality of the city,' The Edge said several years later. 'Dublin and Ireland generally are obviously very influenced by the Catholic church, it's very conservative sexually in terms of advertising, in terms of dress, generally in every way. When I first went to London it was a real buzz, a real rush, because it was such an exciting place.'

Bono's introduction to the city was similar. 'My whole entry into London, going down the tube — all the ads were underpants; neon signs, prostitution, masturbating, people hurrying to get places, traffic going so fast...' For this reason, U2 decided very early on in their career that they would not be moving to London. 'They asked us to, but we said we didn't want to. We don't want to be part of it. I said "No, I don't feel a part of it already, that's not for us."'

U2 signed to the Island label in March, pledging their troth to a company which had long been regarded as one of the most influential, and reputable, in the country. The label had been formed in the early 1960's by Chris Blackwell, as a means of introducing Jamaican music to the United Kingdom, and for three years the company's output — released via a distribution deal with the Fontana label — concentrated on reggae/ska. In 1967, however, Blackwell decided to turn his attention to rock music and, after an initial release by Traffic had proved a major hit, he assembled a roster featuring such bands as King Crimson, Mott The Hoople, Fairport Convention, Emerson Lake And Palmer, and Free — the cream of the British undrground. The inspired signing of Brian Ferry and Roxy Music in 1971, presaged a new era for Island; in June 1974, the company was able to unveil four of its most important recruitments with a show at London's Rainbow Theatre. John Cale, Nico, Kevin Ayres and former Roxy wizard, Brian Eno, were all to figure strongly in the mythology of the punk rock boom which, once again, Island nurtured with such signings as Ultravox and Eddie And The Hot Rods. By 1980, Island could boast acts of the calibre of Suicide, Marianne Faithful and Linton Kwesi Johnson, an élite company to whose ranks many observers felt U2 were privileged to be admitted.

The deal offered U2 the creative freedom they considered so valuable if they were to continue expanding, and a regular wage which finally put paid to two years of scraping by on profits from gigs and, quite literally, the money back on the bottles left behind in the dressing room. 'It sounds like a sad story, but it wasn't. It gave us endurance, I think. We survived on the belief that what we had was important. If we do make money we're look-ing for the fact that we can buy instruments and develop, nothing else. I couldn't care less about money. We've done without it for so long at this stage that it doesn't seem important. We're not thinking about getting married or bringing up kids, that isn't a relevant part of it.'

May saw the release of their first single for the new company; *11 O'Clock Tick Tock*. The song was just one of the forty or so self penned numbers in the band's repertoire, a riveting wall of sound and texture produced by Martin Hannett of Joy Division fame. It was well received by press and public alike, but, in common with the band's next pair of singles, it did not chart.

However, constant gigging in London and around the country saw the band's stock rocketing skywards. 'U2 should establish themselves as one of the best things to come out of Ireland since James Joyce and Guinness,' wrote Melody Maker's Ian Pye in September. That time was getting closer with every passing day.

'U2's live performances have raised their audience's expectations to what must have seemed like an impossible height, but not only have they reached that peak with their first album, they've risen above it,' wrote Melody Maker's Lyndon Barber, reviewing *Boy*. He like so many other people confronted by U2's brilliantly uncompromising debut, went on to proclaim *Boy* one of the finest first albums of all time — joining an élite company which in every poll includes the likes of Roxy Music, The Velvet Underground, Patti Smith

Steve Lillywhite

and The Rolling Stones. In America, especially, the comparisons were numerous. One reviewer placed *Boy* right alongside The Who's *My Generation*, claiming he had had to delve that far back to find an album that affected him in quite the same way.

Boy was recorded at Dublin's Windmill Studios with producer Steve Lillywhite. Then at the very forefront of a new generation of producers, Lillywhite first came to notice when he worked on the debut album by Ultravox, at that time a quite startling hybrid who confidently, but very unfashionably, bridged the gap between early Seventies glam and late Seventies punk. The following year, 1977, Lillywhite produced *Life On The Lines*, the second LP from Southend R&B merchants Eddie And The Hot Rods, and subsequently handled Penetration, the Psychedelic Furs, Toyah, XTC, and the Thompson Twins. Since the termination of his relationship with U2, in 1983, Big Country and Simple Minds have both benefitted from his abilities, couplings which have encouraged a host of 'U2-soundalike' accusations.

In 1980, when he first encountered U2, Lillywhite had just finished producing Peter Gabriel's third, eponymous, album (which included the *Games Without Frontiers* hit single). To switch from a studio veteran such as Gabriel (who by then had been recording for eleven years) to a group as raw and inexperienced as U2 must have presented Lillywhite with quite a challenge. But it was one which he grasped with both hands.

His first session with the band produced their second Island single *A Day Without Me*, and it was immediately apparent that Lillywhite's production techniques were far more in tune with what the band wanted than those of Martin Hannett. Whereas Hannett had concentrated on getting a muted sound, in common with his work with Joy Division, Magazine and John Cooper Clarke, Lillywhite favoured a more open approach.

The album, *Boy,* opened with *I Will Follow*, U2's third Island single and the one which came the closest yet to giving them that first, vital foothold in the chart, not only in Britain, but also in the United States where it became their first single. Riding in on The Edge's

jangling guitar, closely pursued by a thunderous drum sound, *I Will Follow* exploded into view like an atom bomb, a concentrated burst of white light which was not to let up until the album's breathless conclusion. *Stories For Boys*, the track which introduced side two, was just as powerful, its driving beat and soaring guitars the perfect summary of the vitality and delicacy of U2's music. The song was, Bono claimed, an attempt to describe the reactions of a child reading an adventure magazine and realising that life, for him at any rate, was not like that. 'I can remember as a child looking in a mirror and thinking "I don't like that!" It's wrong, you're bombarded with all these images and nobody's like that. The effect is total disillusionment with yourself, you put on a mask and hide from yourself, from your own soul, from what you've got to offer. It's a reaction away from the individual and we stand for individualism.'

Elsewhere, tracks like *Into The Heart, The Electric Company* and, best of all, *An Cat Dubh,* honed down to the barest bones of perfection by months of live work and rehearsal, were singled out for acclaim by critics breathlessly trying to come to terms with what they heard on the record. U2 had only just reached their twentieth birthday, yet their confidence, in terms of playing and delivery, conjured up comparisons with bands five or six years their senior. Tom Verlaine's Television were a favourite reference point for reviewers stuck for an easy categorisation; praise which had flowed so bountifully for that band's *Marquee Moon* album of three years before, was hastily updated and rewritten. And for every critic who felt the need to see U2 comfortably and happily married off to some shadowy legend from rock's cult history, there were two more who could step out and honestly admit that here was a band who were quite unique. U2 had, quite literally, redefined the essence of rock'n'roll for the Eighties. Things could never be the same again.

In other quarters, however, most of the attention was directed not at the music, but at the album's sleeve! It depicted a young boy, naked from the waist up, striking a pose probably more suited to some cheesecake centrefold model. Immediately, accusations of 'child pornography' began to fly at both U2 and the sleeve photographer, Hugo McGuiness. Of course, the furore died away as quickly as it had come, leaving U2 nothing

more than bewildered about the whole affair. The extra publicity generated by the whole debacle could, in fact, have done nothing but aid sales of the record. Nevertheless, *Boy* was unable to breach even the lower reaches of an albums chart which was almost frighteningly devoid of any real competition. At the top, Barbara Streisand and Abba fought it out for supremacy; below them Barry Manilow, George Benson and Johnny Mathis vied for the runners-up slots. And while there can be few people who look towards the Top Fifty for genuine creative inspiration, there was an aching void where some truly contemporary rock music should have been, a void only accentuated by U2's inability to step right into it.

Much of the problem, it was whispered amongst the rock cognoscenti, lay in the massive media build-up which U2 had received. As Kris Needs of ZigZag had observed earlier in the year, U2 were '...a Hot New Band. But there are loads of Hot New Bands...one every month to build up by rave press, a buzz stoked up by gigs, the first vinyl released to acclaim...and then it ain't a Hot New Band, but a cabaret act expected to do three tours a year, play the ones they know and do periodic records to fulfill the contract.' And, Needs continued, when they finally split or fell from grace, '...there's always two more hydra-heads to replace them.'

'What can happen is that you turn like a circle instead of a spiral,' Bono countered. 'We look at a spiral so that we can get higher. I look at it like a tower with people all around. If you're at the bottom, only the ones nearest can hear. You've got to climb higher for more people to hear, for those further back. It's just as important to reach those people, they might have heard less good music, have nine to five jobs. I think success and building it up is important, you must always climb. It can be a routine to climb, but I see it like a spiral, getting higher...'

And as for the accusations of hype; 'I don't feel we have been hyped by the music press because I happen to agree with the good things they say about us. The music press' relationship with U2 has meant that a lot of people come along expecting a lot and they've got a lot, sometimes maybe too much. It is a pressure, but if people come along expecting the world from U2, then they're gonna get it. I'm not scared that we won't be able to give it to them.'

Below: The Virgin Prunes. Dik is third from the left

CHAPTER TWO
SECONDS

The beginning of 1980 saw the debut of an interesting off-shoot from the U2 'family'. Another Dublin band, The Virgin Prunes, released their debut record in January, an EP called *Twenty Tens.* And for people whose most recent exposure to the sound of the city had been the *Just For Kicks* album and the Boomtown Rats' *Fine Art Of Surfacing,* the Prunes' excursions far beyond the realms of either rock fashion or credibility came as something of a shock.

The Prunes and U2 had grown up together in Dublin or, as they preferred to claim, Lipton Village. 'It's an imaginary place, somewhere we developed in our imaginations to give us an alternative lifestyle as kids,' Bono says. 'We grew up studying people on street corners. We laughed at the way they talked and at the expressions they made. We mocked the adult world and agreed we would never grow up because all we saw was silliness.'

The close relations between the two bands have been fostered by Dik, the Prune's guitarist, being The Edge's brother. Also, the boy whose photograph appears on the covers of both *Boy* and *War* is the younger brother of Guggi, at that time the Prunes' vocalist; Guggi himself was so christened by Bono. 'It has something to do with my ugliness,' Guggi explains modestly.

However close the two bands might be socially, musically they are worlds apart, as American audiences discovered when the Prunes toured the United States in the wake of U2's own breakthrough there. They were billed as 'Friends of U2', a subtle ploy by local promoters to attract houses as full as those which greeted U2 — although, in fairness, it is unlikely that many of these promotors actually knew what they would be getting themselves into. Rumours even spread that the Prunes *were* U2 and that the short string of dates were a secret prelude to U2's own, next assault on the land.

Such advertising worked well — for ten minutes. Then, according to witnesses, the audience would walk out en masse, leaving the Prunes to play on to a handful of curious onlookers who still believed that sooner or later this bizzare bunch would quit clowning around and start playing songs. The reaction when they didn't must have pleased the Prunes no end.

'We want our audiences to do as they wish,' Gavin Strongman told ZigZag's Tom Vague. 'Listen or throw bottles, it's up to them, not us. They can make their own minds up.' Dave-d Busaras Scott added; 'Society is to blame for our performance.'

Perhaps unsurprisingly, the Virgin Prunes have never made a major breakthrough, either in America or Britain. But for U2, the day of reckoning was closing in fast. Wooed by reports from the band's gigs back in the spring (especially the March, 1980 Acklam

Hall show, where U2 had been supported by the Prunes and fellow Dubliners, Berlin) and the intermittent dates since then, audiences turned out in their droves when tickets went on sale for U2's first major headlining tour of Britain. It began in September, with a second billing to Echo & The Bunnymen at London's Lyceum, and continued on for two months, encompassing a very prestigious weekly residency at the Marquee Club. In October, between British dates, U2 made their European debut in Belgium and Holland; in December they paid their first visit to the United States, with a short tour of the East Coast. In February, readers of the New Musical Express voted U2 the sixth 'Best New Act' of the year; that same month, over seven hundred people were locked out of the London Lyceum; inside, U2 and their support act, The Thompson Twins, were playing to a rapturous, capacity crowd.

And finally, in August, *Boy* entered the album chart and, although it eventually peaked at the relatively low position of number fifty-two, it was to remain on the listings for over two months. It also made the American Top 100, albeit at number ninety-four.

U2 had returned to the United States in April. Their first visit to the country the previous autumn, like those first UK gigs had been a fact-finding mission, testing the water before a more concerted effort was made. The spring 1982 tour saw U2 leaving the East Coast and striking out into other areas; places like Dallas where, in a scene probably more suited to the television series, the band's request that they be paid in cash was met by the promoter drawing his gun and, after a few moments thought, answering in the negative. They would be paid by cheque, like everybody else.

'The American thing has taken off so fast,' Larry told Melody Maker's Paolo Hewitt, when

he caught up with the band in Chicago. 'We started off playing the small clubs and on the next half of this tour we're playing really big places, places the Boomtown Rats are playing!'.

The tour included two dates in New York; the first, a sell-out at The Ritz, was described by Melody Maker's David Fricke as '...an intense five star performance that bodes well for (U2's) chances in this country.' The second, at the Palladium, saw U2 sharing a double billing with the Liverpool group, Teardrop Explodes.

Producer Steve Lillywhite joined the band in America for the last month of the tour. U2 were gradually working their latest material into the live set, and the excursion was the perfect opportunity for Lillywhite to become familiar with the new songs before he and U2 returned to Dublin to begin work on the band's second album. As a rehearsal of sorts, the party used a break in the touring schedule to visit the Compass Point studios in Nassau. It was here that Island stablemates Talking

Heads, the Tom Tom Club and Robert Palmer regularly recorded, and U2 joined this illustrious company by laying down their own new single at the studio. *Fire* was released in July 1981, U2's first British single in almost nine months, and at long last U2 found themselves with a hit.

To aid promotion, Island dreamed up the idea of a double-pack single; two records for the price of one. A limited edition was released which, besides the regular 'a' and 'b' sides, included a bonus live disc. The added sales incentive was, no doubt, very instrumental in *Fire's* rise to just outside the top thirty.

In October, U2 released their second album. Originaly to be titled *Scarlet,* the set was now dubbed *October,* a title which, like the discarded *Scarlet,* came from one of the tracks on the album; in this instance, a short and haunting ballad which was quite at odds with anything U2 had done in the past. Instead of

The Edge's liquid guitar there was a sensitive piano arrangement; where Bono had once cried to the skies he was now mournful, almost melancholic. It was a beautifully evocative piece of music and only one of several tracks on the album which saw U2 making dramatic departures away from the sound which had heralded their arrival in the rock arena. *October* was an infinitely more accomplished album than its predecessor. *Boy,* by comparison, now seemed clumsy in places; sometimes tentative, even nervous. The band now skipped blithely over arrangements which demonstrated just how much U2 had progressed, both in terms of presentation and dynamics.

Much of the difference, Bono claimed, lay in the age of the songs. Most of *Boy* had been written during the band's earliest days — even *11 O'Clock Tick Tock,* one of the most recent songs on the set, dated back to the spring of 1980 when U2 supported Talking Heads at the Electric Ballroom in London.

'...I didn't really know what I was talking about,' Bono admitted later. 'I just had feelings about things. Now I feel stronger as a person. We've been everywhere; we've seen half the world in the last eight months. We've had to deal with every sort of angle of business through record companies.' He described *Boy* as an album of moods, abstracted and, because of the ideas that went into it, somehow illogical. *October* was a far stronger statement of intent.

'That album was made under a lot of pressure. I remember writing lyrics at the microphone and at £50 an hour that's quite a pressure. Lillywhite was pacing up and down the studio ...he coped really well. And the ironic thing about *October* is that there is a sort of peace about the album even though it was recorded under that pressure.'

It was, in fact, the pressures which contributed so much to *October's* quite extraordinary atmosphere. Whereas so many bands deliver up a stunning debut album, then find themselves devoid of both material and inspiration for material when it comes to recording the follow up, this punishing schedule provided U2 with a new impetus to come up with a music that was fresh and vital. They could not rest on their laurels, bathing in the critical acclaim which still surrounded *Boy.* Having spent so much time since that album's release on the road, they had been subject to external stimuli which many bands just never encounter, particularly at such an early stage of their career. The pressures of having to record so quickly after coming off the road meant that the new material and ideas had no time to stagnate.

Paradoxically, *October* was a long way from the 'life on the road and other stories' album which U2 would have been so well qualified to make. Its over-riding theme was that of faith. Despite Bono's oft-repeated assertions that he is 'all but anti-religious', there was never any denying that faith was one of the most important ingredients in U2, although 'not everyone in the band believes the same way. I think people understand that I'm not religious — when I talk of religion I'm talking about the force which has cut this country (Ireland) in two. I'm not religious at all, but I do believe in God very strongly and I don't believe that we just kind of exploded out of thin air, I can't believe it.

'I think it's the spiritual strength that's essential to the band. People have got to find their own way. I'm not into standing up and saying "Hey! You should be into God!" My own life is exhilarating through an experience I feel, and there's no point in talking about something which should be there in your life anyway. You don't have to preach about it... There are things I don't want to talk about... wherever you look, in the Catholic church and Protestant church, you see flaws. You can't ever find purity or perfection and we find ourselves becoming more and more distanced. We get flak from all sides, really heavy letters from people saying "How can you believe this and do this?" I'll talk about (those things) in the music.'

Gloria, which opened the album, put these emotions into music. Anthemic, the song was described by one critic as being the nearest rock music has ever come to producing a hymn; 'but not a hymn in the church sense, rather in the sense that it is uplifting, spiritual, a song of praise and glory, of power and love.' On a more concrete level, *Gloria* remains an in-concert favourite, its soaring melodies and fragile guitar lines being a perfect foil for the massed singalongs which U2 audiences specialise in and which, once again, indicate a potency in the song which is far removed from the custom-built rabble rousing so beloved by many of U2's contemporaries.

Rejoice, further on in the album, reiterates this power in a reaffirmation of the band's belief in the importance of faith. Its title was a recurrent motif throughout the album; the

lyric to *Scarlet*, for instance, consisted solely of the one word repeated over and over. This repetition of a word unsettled many people and many critics intimated, made *October* a difficult album to grow accustomed to, something which Bono was quick to agree with.

'I used the word "Rejoice" precisely because I know that people have a mental block against it. It's a powerful word. It's lovely to say. It's implying more than simply "Get up and dance, baby". I think that *October* goes into areas that most rock and roll bands ignore. When I listen to that record it actually moves me.'

Yet, at the time it was made and for a long while afterwards, Bono claims that he could not bring himself to even play *October* because he didn't fully understand it. When the album came out, U2 even made a concerted attempt *not* to talk to the music press about it; an unprecedented move. In February 1982, with the album four months in the shops, Bono told Melody Maker's Lynden Barber; '*October* is now much clearer in my head. I listened to it for the first time in ages last week and I couldn't believe I was part of it. It's a huge record, I couldn't cope with it.'

If *Gloria* and *Rejoice* spearheaded the spiritual side of *October*, *I Fall Down* and *Fire* were more aggressive, harkening back to the garage land roar of the first album. At that

time, Bono described the group's sound as dealing with the confusion and ignorance of adolescence; 'Out of that confusion comes a semblance of what you're trying to find yourself. It can be a very explosive time, so a lot of the songs deal with that sort of struggle. I use the image of twilight, because it's grey… things are hard to see. There's confusion. You're fighting against it all the time.' This imagery surfaced in *Twilight And Tall Trees* (a title borrowed from the seventh chapter of William Golding's Lord Of The Flies novel) on *Boy,* and Bono returned to it on *October. I Threw A Brick Through A Window* portrayed the hunger of a sixteen year old '…seeing a reflection of yourself in a window and seeing who you are just for a split second and realising you don't like what you see.'

He talked about how being a member of U2 had altered his view of himself: 'I've changed as it's gone through. When it started I was very drunk on being in a band, very confident. It was everything. I couldn't see the wood for the trees. You get bitter, you knock other bands. I had a lot of hate…

'That's changed in my life. U2 has broadened my experience, allowed me to realise that wherever you go in the world people are still flesh and blood, that wherever you go people are being cheated.'

It was this experience which allowed the band to write songs like *Stranger In A Strange Land,* an epic of alienation which borrowed its title from a novel by Robert Heinlein, and the closing *Is That All?*, two songs which, in their subtle use of light and shade, their alternation between delicacy and strength, served as a self-styled reference point for the group's future direction. Ideas and textures which U2 had introduced on *Boy* were now taken to their logical conclusions and, although the progressions would not be truly complete for another eighteen months, with *October* U2 were very audibly aligning themselves with peaks of musical achievement which displayed a firm commitment to destinies totally at odds with the preconceptions of their audience. Working against what were accepted as the boundaries of rock fashion, U2's detachment from the rock mainstream was creating a whole new approach to their goals — an approach which, in the words of the New Musical Express' Gavin Martin, was soon to spawn a whole generation of little U2's, bastard surrogates who, in the guise of returning the guitar anthem to its 'rightful' place in the rock hierarchy, were inadvertently missing the entire point. U2's approach was all about individuality, an approach nurtured by the band having spent their apprenticeship in Dublin as opposed to London, Birmingham or some other mainland city where the indigenous music scene is as reliant on on-going fashions as the national scene. Away from the limelight and the tribalism which inevitably accompanies it, U2 had been able to develop at their own speed, taking their career forward one step at a time. 'A lot of bands just stumble up the stairs and tumble down again', Bono said. 'We're building. We believe in what we do.' It was this belief which characterised both *Boy* and *October,* which made them at once vastly accessible at the same time as being deeply personal. The band played to their own individuality; as The Edge was to say; 'We're not a punk band, ska or whatever. Just U2'.

Bono added; 'What we have in this band is special. The sound might be classical, but it is naturally our own. We don't sound like any other group. Our songs are different. They hold emotions of a spiritual nature.'

Yet the autumn of 1981 was not, in top fifty terms at least, a particularly appropriate time to talk of such qualities. Novelty music was the order of the day, 'acts' such as Joe Dolce, The Tweets and Aneka took a chunk of chart action way out of proportion to their talent. Adam and the Ants ruled supreme, their jukebox tribal chants setting new standards in Panto-rock, while a mercifully brief nation-wide obsession with medley-hits, led by the Dutch Starsound combo, seemingly spelled the end of the three minute tune for ever; now tunes could be condensed to three seconds and full length songs existed only to give the guilty men more options when it came to piecing together their next master-piece. The Human League's *Dare,* a brutal distilling of all that group had once held dear, was the country's best selling LP. Into this climate U2 plunged *October,* an album as thoughtful as its competitors were banal, as melodic as others were dirgelike. But for everybody who thought U2 had something to say there were hundreds more who thought 'Shakey' said it just as well, and *October,* for all its beauty and strength could rise no higher than eleventh place, although sales eventually topped 250,000; enough to earn U2 a silver disc. It was an impressive showing by the band's own standards, but to the outside observer, watching U2's progress with a coldly dispassionate eye, it was hard to see just what the band's supporters had to get so excited about.

October might have fared better had the band been as available as they'd been during the previous year. For much of the 1981, U2 were based exclusively in the United States. In November, they arrived for their third tour in twelve months, facing a jaunt around venues whose capacity often approached 3,000 people. And it was all down to their own hard work. Just as, in Britain, U2 had steadily built up their reputation, playing gigs, getting rebooked and drawing larger crowds, inching their way further up the ladder, so American audiences were quick to reward a band who were not scared to leave the big cities and head out for the smaller communities, the deep South and the Mid-West, areas where only the most hardened of visiting bands would even dream of venturing.

Neither was American radio slow to pick up on this latest live phenomenon. Not the major AM/Commercial stations, of course; for them there is no life beyond the national top forty. The more progressive minded stations, though, college stations and local FM concerns, treated U2 as a godsend. Here was a band who eschewed the soundalike conventions of what was normally termed rock music and were not afraid to go out on a limb, yet who remained instantly accessible to anybody who cared to listen. When U2 were in town, the airwaves would be saturated with their music; on their November 1982 tour, for instance, U2's gig at the 2,500 seater Boston Orpheum was broadcast live, in its entirety, by the local WBCN station, one of the most popular and most influential in the whole New England area.

In January, 1982, U2 played their first Irish dates in well over a year. They were so popular in their homeland at this point that only the largest venues in Ireland could accommodate them; the tour, then, amounted to just three dates in the Republic; Galway, Cork and Dublin. A solitary show in Belfast was cancelled when the venue's floor collapsed shortly before the date. Nevertheless, around ten thousand people were able to see the band, half of them at the massive Royal Dublin Society hall, a concert which Melody Maker described as '...a symbolic homecoming...U2 transformed this massive cowshed into an uninhibited exhibition of joy (which) has to be experienced to be believed.'

The celebrations were made complete when national RTE disc jockey Dave Fanning announced the results of his late night rock show listener's poll. In a chart of fifty 'All Time Classics', U2 took six places, including the number one slot. *11 O'Clock Tick Tock* was the most popular rock song in Eire.

In April, U2 released their next single. *Celebration,* backed by the improvised *Trash Trampoline And Party Girl,* reached number forty-seven in the UK chart, its appearance putting paid to rumours that U2 had dropped producer Steve Lillywhite. Speculation had grown following the band's brief studio sojourn with the legendary American producer, Sandy Pearlman. Best known for his work with the likes of Pavlov's Dog, The Dictators and the Blue Oyster Cult, Pearlman had been admired by U2 since they heard *Give 'Em Enough Rope,* the 1978 album which coupled The Clash with Pearlman.

'We wanted to get away from the cinematic sound,' explained Bono, holding The Clash's second album up as an example of Pearlman's abilities to tap the rawness so vital to any band. However, the union did not survive. U2 recorded just one track with Pearlman, a 'psychobilly' number which remains incomplete to this day. A forty-eight track studio had been needed, but neither band or producer had access to anything larger than twenty-four.

'I liked him,' Bono said later. 'When we were on tour he followed us everywhere, flying from city to city. He was just like a fan.'

Lillywhite, then, was booked to oversee the sessions for U2's next album; these began in August. Over the preceding months, the band played a string of festival dates across Europe, most notably the Werchter Festival, in Belgium. U2 appeared alongside Simple Minds, Peter Gabriel and The Eurythmics in an event which was filmed and recorded by Belgium's ID television and film company. U2's sound was mixed by Lillywhite, and excerpts from the show appeared both on the flip of their next single and on a very high quality bootleg, titled simply *U2: Live.*

Also in July, U2 played their first British date of 1982, appearing second billed to The Police at the Gateshead International Stadium. Perhaps the most important gig of all, though, was at the fifth birthday party for Dublin's Hot Press, a rock magazine which has championed U2's cause since the band's inception. It was not the biggest gig U2 have ever played, neither was it the most prestigious. But to Dubliners, people who had watched as U2 rose from the local pub circuit to international stadiums and festivals, it was a sure sign that the band had not lost touch with their roots. And that meant a lot.

CHAPTER THREE
WAR FEVER

'When we were making that LP we went practically to the point of breaking up the band. When we go into the studio we draw totally on our deepest resources and stretch them to the limit. If a band is going to be honest, they've got to bring out everything, even the things that frighten them.'

In February, 1983, U2 released their third album. It smashed straight into the chart at number one (the twenty-fourth album to do so this decade) and stayed in the chart for over a year. Today it stands as one of the most successful albums of the 1980s. It was called *War*.

'War seemed to be the motif for 1982. Everywhere you looked, from the Falklands to the Middle East to South Africa, there was war. By calling the new album *War*, we're giving people a slap in the face and, at the same time, getting away from the cosy image a lot of people have of U2.'

War was harsh and hard, uncompromising and uncomfortable. Where the band could have played safe, they went out on to the ledge, peered into the abyss and jumped right in. '*War* is a heavy title, it's blunt. It could backfire,' admitted The Edge. 'It's the sort of subject matter that people can really take a dislike to, but we wanted to take a more dangerous course, fly a bit closer to the wind, so I think the title is appropriate.'

Celebration, U2's single of the previous spring, had set the stage. Bono had sung of

his belief in a third world war, his belief in the atom bomb, knowing full well that the immediate assumption, however misconceived it may be, would be that the band were condoning the things they sung about. They didn't; 'That song was a pointer. It showed our idealism was not becoming dissipated.' It showed that U2 were prepared to face up to the realities of life in the post-nuclear Eighties. In the past, U2 admit, they had been accused, and rightfully so, of abstraction, of dealing in ambiguities and skirting around the issues that really mattered. *War* saw them taking the opposite stance, grabbing the bull by the horns, wrestling not only with their own emotions, but those of their whole generation as well. The images were of Northern Ireland, of Afghanistan, of a world held to ransom by a D.I.Y. bomb builder. You can make them anywhere, sang Bono. The plans are available in any public reference library, all you need is a slightly more than rudimentary knowledge of physics and a few hundred pounds worth of raw materials. Then back to your apartment in Times Square… That was *Seconds*, a vivid montage which was surpassed in potency only by the opening number *Sunday, Bloody Sunday*.

U2 had always steered clear of writing abut Northern Ireland in the past; in fact, according to Bono; 'It was only going to America made us think about Ireland. You don't think about

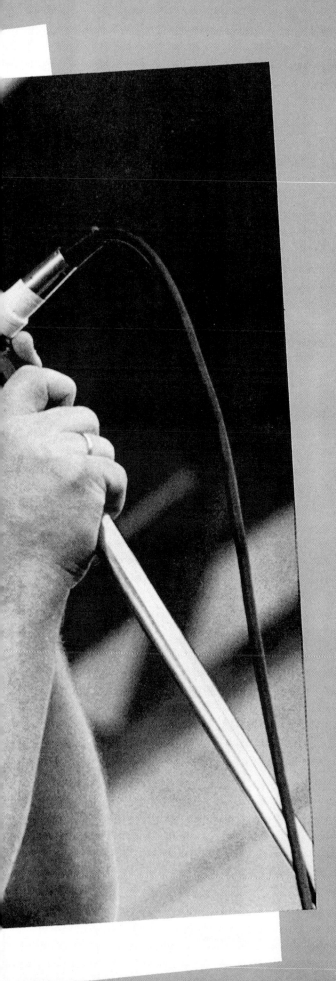

it until you have people throwing money on stage during Bobby Sands and the whole hunger strike thing. I thought that guy must be so brave, but why? Why be brave? Why die? There's something not right about this. People were going; "Yeah! You're Irish!"'

But, he continued, people were seeing Ireland in black and white, stark right and wrong, '...and they didn't realise it was all in the grey. Having had a Protestant father and a Catholic mother, I know how grey it is. There are no sides (and) I think people know better now, having met people since the LP. I think we've contributed to that understanding.'

There was, of course, nothing new in a group singing about the Irish 'troubles'. John Lennon, Paul McCartney and the Sutherland Brothers are just three of the artists to have committed their views on the subject to vinyl; Lennon even wrote a song called *Sunday, Bloody Sunday,* back in 1972, a song which dealt in no uncertain terms with the Easter Day uprising of 1916. U2's song of that name was less overtly political than that of their illustrious predecessor; nonetheless, the band felt obliged to give it a 'trial run' in front of a native audience before making the final decision to include it on the album. Says The Edge; 'It's very hard for us to justify a title like that. All we can say is that we're trying to confront the subject rather than sweep it under the carpet. We thought a lot about that song before we played it in Belfast. Bono told the audience that if they didn't like it then we would never play it again. Out of the three thousand people in the hall, about three walked out. I think that says a lot about the audience's trust in us.'

Sunday, Bloody Sunday was not, as was believed by many people on both sides of the Atlantic, a song about '...the troubles in the physical sense of the fighting.' According to Adam, it dealt with '...the human carnage of families being wrecked.' U2 were taking no sides because, as they have continually found themselves saying, there aren't any sides to take. Bono says; 'I would like to see a united Ireland (because) I believe it is an island. People then say "do you believe in a cause enough to die for it?" I believe in a cause enough to live for it. These people believe in taking other people's lives away. I just can not agree with this whole "If you don't agree with me I'll put a gun to your head" vibe.' There are no sides, and ultimately there are no solutions. *Sunday, Bloody Sunday* is *not* a rebel song.

It is, however, one of the most emotive rock songs even written. Above a driving military tattoo, Bono's voice strains with a tension which, he admits, he never knew he possessed. Steve Wickham's biolin adds a new, manic dimension to the sound, weaving insanely through the regimented rhythms of the song's coda. It could, as several people have suggested, quite possibly be the single most important song of the last ten years.

Yet despite the political implications, not only of *Sunday Bloody Sunday*, but the entire *War* concept, U2 remain staunchly apolitical. Unlike so many other bands in their position, U2 have never regarded their ability to reach tens of thousands of people as a way in which to force their own personal opinions across. For them, the stage is just that, a stage. It is not a pulpit, U2 are not preachers. 'There are a lot of people who say I get up on soap boxes,' Bono told the audience at the first night of U2's 1983 British tour. 'This is untrue. I've never had any time for soap boxes.' He describes the white flag which was unfurled on stage during *Sunday, Bloody Sunday* merely as '...a symbolic gesture. I was sick of the green, white and orange, I was sick of the Union Jack, I was sick of the Stars and Stripes. I wished all the colours could be drained from

them and just leave the white flag. And I felt that a lot of people wanted that to be said, a lot of people who were in our audience.'

On a later date, he was honest enough to admit; 'The best way we can contribute to our time and our generation is just getting down to what we do, which is make records. Although we can lend our support to things like CND, these things are all inherently flawed.'

U2 did, in fact, pledge themselves to speak for CND in Ireland; they were not adverse to playing occasional benefit gigs either. A December 1984 show at New York's Radio City Hall, for instance, was designed to raise funds for Amnesty International (not, as the Radio City security guards seemed to think, to give the venue's hired muscle an opport-unity to beat up any member of the audience who got too close to the stage). The band also involved themselves in the quiet funding of local Dublin community ventures although, as The Edge said; 'There are ways we can do things, but we must never be seen as a charity, the noble boys doling out the slops. Just keep our mouths shut and get things done.'

It was for these reasons that Bono declined an offer from Irish premier, Garrett Fitzgerald, to lend his support to a committee being set up to investigate youth unemployment in Eire. Bono had first met Fitzgerald shortly before

the latter took office; they had an half hour argument at Heathrow Airport, whilst waiting for a flight to Dublin. The argument continued on to the plane home. 'It was not in an aggressive way,' Bono later explained. 'I was asking him why politicians don't speak the language of the people, why they invented their own language which leaves the rest of the country out. I was saying that any leader of a country had to throw away the political language that they had and speak to the people.'

Fizgerald contacted Bono again, during the recording of *War*. 'I'd been mouthing off to him about unemployment, (so) he said "Well, we're putting together this emergency committee on unemployment and I want you on it." And I said; "What can I do?" Essentially, I was (to be) a troublemaker. All I could do was arrive at these meetings and when people said "What young people feel like..." I'd say: "Hey! I'm one of them."

'But I realised that I wasn't unempoyed. I realised that I didn't want to speak at a committee meeting about rape without someone raped being with me, didn't want to speak about unemployment without some-one unemployed with me. I realised there was another language, committee-speak, and I didn't understand that. I didn't speak the language.

The release of *War* was heralded with several singles. On the continent, *Sunday, Bloody Sunday* was culled from the set, but the song was considered too inflammatory for release in the United Kingdom, if only because it seemed unlikely that the BBC would ever play it. Instead, *New Year's Day* was put out. An acknowledgement of Poland's outlawed Solidarity movement, *New Year's Day* was a somewhat pessimistic observation of the fact that, no matter how hard people try to change a situation, things are always basically the same at the begin-ning of every new year. What U2 could not have known when they wrote the song was that January 1st, 1983, would become a landmark in the short and turbulent history of Solidarity, for it was on that day that the Polish government lifted the martial law imposed in the wake of the Solidarity riots.

The single was given the full benefit of Island's marketing strength. Three different variations on the single were released; a conventional 7" disc; a double pack, featuring three live cuts (recorded at the Werchter Festival); and a 12" single, which again included three live tracks. The most interest-ing song, however, was *Treasure*, a studio recording which was subtitled *Whatever Happened To Pete The Chop?* Pete The Chop was a friend of U2 from their earliest days in Dublin who, one day, asked Bono to write a hit single about him. *Treasure* was the result and its arrival into the upper echelons of the chart on the 'b' side of *New Year's Day* finally fulfilled a three year old prophecy by Kris Needs, of ZigZag magazine. In June, 1980, he wrote; 'One day the bloke who calls him-self Pete The Chop may find his moniker immortalised in the top ten.'

A second single from *War, Two Hearts Beat As One*, was released in March. Again it came in three different formats, but this time around, U2 could only scrape into the lower reaches of the top twenty, despite the added incentive of remixed versions of both *New Year's Day* and *Two Hearts* on the single's flip. Despite the band's stranglehold on the American new wave rock audience, they were having some difficulty establishing them-selves in the dance clubs; an area which has become vital to European rock acts in the States. U2 records were played, but up against artists such as Soft Cell and New Order, bands who not only released their singles in extended formats, but who often commissioned special, new dance mixes for the clubs. U2 were coming in a very poor second. Therefore, Island boss Chris Blackwell took the master tapes of both *New Year's Day* and *Two Hearts Beat As One* to remix specialist Francas Kervorkian, a man whose biggest ambition, according to Bono, is to remix Jemi Hendrix. 'So Chris gave him what he considered the next best thing — The Edge.'

Unlike his contemporaries in the remixing business, Kervorkian steers clear of over-dubbing new instruments and sound effects onto his project. Instead, he works with the materials at hand, making the song more 'acceptable' to new markets without ever altering the band's original handiwork. His revamping of *Two Hearts Beat As One*, for instance, concentrated on accentuating the song's natural dance rhythms, a process which was rewarded when the remix became one of the most requested songs in the new wave dance clubs of America.

Critical reaction to *War* was mixed. Melody Maker's Adam Sweeting pointed out that, while the songs dealt with the struggle for peace, the sound was very militaristic. Bono countered the accusation by claiming that the album was intended to convey an impression of 'militant pacifism. That's what Martin Luther King was, he wasn't a passive pacifist, he was a militant pacifist... With *Boy* and *October* I got flak because they were so abstract. So with *War* I decided to strip it right down. I can see how it might have sounded like a finger pointing (but) we've never pointed a finger at anybody except ourselves. It can come across like I'm angry at the audience, it's always *us* with U2. I never write songs about "you" or "they", it's "us" or "we" or "I". Always. It's a big difference.

'I think it's a more pompous thing rather than pretentious. Usually it's because... coming from Ireland you're a bit like (aggressive) so people ask you a question and it's Bop! and it came across as being a little heavy at times. But I never point a finger... sometimes the tone of my voice gives the impression of a warning, but I never

the **unforgettable FIRE**

First United States Exhibition of Original Drawings by Survivors of the Hiroshima and Nagasaki Bombings

August 6–November 30, 1982 • Opening Friday, August 6, 6:00–10:00 p.m.

The **PEACE MUSEUM**
gallery resource center workshop

364 W. Erie, Chicago • 440-1860

Hours: Noon–5 Tues., Wed., Fri., Sat., Sun., noon–8 Thurs.
Adults $1.00, children under 12 and senior citizens 50¢
Group tours welcome

point.'

War made the top ten in America, and as in Britain, it was a performance which more than belied previous chart placings. *October* had peaked at ninety-four in the U.S. just one place above *Boy*. U2 returned to America on completion of a twenty-eight date British tour (including four London dates) in February. 'We love being in America as far as playing is concerned,' Bono said. 'The audience reaction is instinctive. There isn't much reading on music. The only way people hear about things is by radio, which is very localised. You could be huge in Boston and people won't have heard of you in Texas.'

This time around U2's schedule consisted almost exclusively of major festival sites and football stadiums, the logical conclusion to the band's steady rise up the American concert circuit. Bruce Springsteen attended one show in Philadelphia; Bono dedicated the encore to Steel Mill, one of Springsteen's early bands. The peak came in June, when the band headlined the enormous outdoor Red Rocks festival, in Denver, Colorado. The stage was set in a natural amphitheatre in the rocks, the arena lit up by strategically placed bonfires. It was one of the largest, and most ambitious events of its kind ever staged anywhere in the world; subsequent video, television and record sales established it as one of the most lucrative as well.

The tour over, U2 donated their War backdrop and stage set to the Chicago Peace Museum. It was exhibited along side a series of paintings, Japanese art treasures, painted by survivors of the two atomic blasts at Hiroshima and Nagasaki. The collection was titled *The Unforgettable Fire*.

CHAPTER FOUR
A SORT OF HOMECOMING

At the end of November, Island released the live album *Under A Blood Red Sky.* It had been recorded on the band's world tour of that summer and, despite the advertising which tied the record up with the Red Rock gig, only two tracks on the LP *Gloria* and *Trash Trampoline And Party Girl* actually came from that particular show. The remainder of the set was culled from performances in Boston, Mass., and Germany's Rockpalast television show.

There were several reasons for the release, not least a desire on the part of Island to keep U2 in the public eye and — with Christmas so close — the public pocket. There was also the perrenial problem of bootlegging. Since 1981, when the 'problem' had first raised its head, illicit recordings of U2, taken from either live performances or radio broadcasts, had proliferated to the extent that one dealer was able to boast that he had shifted almost two hundred cassette tapes of U2's 1983 Hammersmith Palais performance in the month immediately following the show.

Since bootlegs first appeared on the scene, in the late sixties with a two record set of Bob Dylan's legendary *Basement Tapes*, bands, record companies and copyright authorities had tried their utmost to rid the world of what they considered a most evil cancer. But, undeterred by numerous prosecutions, the bootleggers continue to flourish and the advent of small, easily portable cassette recorders have made their task even easier.

Tapes and records, often of equal quality to 'official' releases can be found at any street market or record fair, while the classified advertisement columns in the music press, despite strongly worded warnings about the illegitimacy of such enterprising, overflow with scarcely concealed offers of 'rare/live/imports' by just about every major (or minor) band imaginable.

The objections to bootlegging are, of course, easily justified. First and foremost, there is the loss of revenue involved. An artist receives no payment for material used in this way, but, argue the bootleggers, since very little of what appears on bootleg would ever see the light of day in any other form, the artist would not receive any money for it anyway. At least this way he gets some extra publicity!

The second major objection relates to the lack of quality control. Few bootleggers would ever hold back from selling a tape of a bad gig, or even a tape that, through the use of inadequate recording equipment or tapes, is all but unlistenable. A flood of such obviously sub-standard material can only damage an artist's reputation. The argument to that is equally obvious. The majority of people who buy bootlegs are fans of the artist anyway; they have no need to have the artist's reputation clarified for them, but every need to hear the artist under whatever conditions possible.

It is unlikely that such claims and counter

claims will ever be resolved, and for many bands, the easiest way of stemming the flow of unofficial product is to release a live album of their own. The Rolling Stones did it in 1970, when their most recent American tour was surfacing on vinyl right across the western world. Nils Lofgren did it six years later, taking the ball right into the bootlegger's own court when he christened the limited edition radio promotional disc *An Authorised Bootleg*; paradoxically, this album swiftly became so in-demand that bootlegs of the bootleg followed with almost indecent haste.

Under A Blood Red Sky's effect on the private market will never be gauged; suffice to say that there was no appreciable lessening of trade for the bootleggers, despite the album's almost unprecedented success. Selling at a very modest £2.99 (with U2 taking a substantial cut in their royalties to make that possible), *Under A Blood Red Sky* entered the chart at number nine, rocketing to the top slot the following week. It was eventually awarded a platinum disc, one of the very few live albums ever to have sold over one million copies in this country.

Six months later, Virgin videos released *Live At Red Rocks Under A Blood Red Sky*. This *had* been shot at the festival, a lengthier version of the film shown on Channel 4's Midsummer Night's Tube the previous year. As a documentary of the band in concert it could scarecely be faulted, as a piece of cinema verité it was one of the most convincing examples of the genre rock'n'roll has ever spawned. Every camera technique imaginable, from stage front close ups to magnificent panaramas of the entire arena (shot from a helicopter) was employed; Jack Barron, reviewing the video in Sounds claimed that it '...captures the atmosphere of a live gig as well as any I can think of.'

The Edge was rather more disparaging, particularly when questioned about the visual aspects of the film. '(That) owes a lot to the weather being so bad. If the sun had been shining I'm sure that the video would be okay,' he said, although he also conceded that a bright and sunny day '...wouldn't suit the group in the way it (the bad weather) does.' Indeed, it was the fact that the weather *was* so bad that made the video such an impressive sight. The air was ringing wet, giving the lights a misty, ethereal quality which a clear night could never have managed. The fires, reflecting off the water, were spectacular; in fact, as Barron pointed out in his review, the

best thing about *Under A Blood Red Sky* was that '...you don't have to get sopping wet, unlike the people who attended.'

Throughout the summer of 1984, U2 were ensconced within the walls of Slane Castle, an imposing stately home in County Meath, where they were recording their latest album under the aegis of Brian Eno and his partner, Daniel Lanois. It was a coupling which raised more than a few eyebrows. Here were U2, the epitome of rock'n'roll, being supervised by Eno, the man behind a string of 'ambient' records, soothing background muzak which its creator best summed up when he titled albums; *Music For Airports, Music For Films* and *Discreet Music*. Eno's relationship with rock music has always been very tenuous; apart from his involvement with Roxy Music and a brace of highly idiosyncratic solo albums in the early to mid Seventies, he has preferred to tackle the genre purely through the medium of other people's work; David Bowie's *Low/Heroes/Lodger* trilogy, the Talking Heads *More Songs About Buildings And Food/Fear Of Music/Remain In Light*

trilogy and a collaboration with Heads' vocalist David Byrne; *My Life In The Bush Of Ghosts.* He told Melody Maker, shortly after completing work with U2; 'I'm not really interested in being a producer, it's not my main thing at all.' He did, in fact, admit that he had had doubts about working with U2, eventually succumbing because; 'I felt I had a lot to learn from it. I also knew it was a pretty controversial job when I decided on it and I suppose that too appealed to me.

'I was mystified by their reasons for wanting me particularly, I wanted to discover just what it was they wanted from me.'

According to The Edge; 'When we were deciding on a producer for this record, his (Eno's) name kept coming up. I mean, within the band there's quite a variety of different tastes in music and producers and what have you, but whenever Brian's name was brought up it seemed to meet with unanimous approval.'

Brian Eno

The band had, in fact, been contemplating producing the record themselves, something which they had not done since those first two singles in Ireland. The names of Bert Whelan and Jimmy Iovine cropped up too. Whelan had produced *Refugee,* one of the cuts on *War,* Iovine — best known for his work with Patti Smith, Tom Petty, and Dire Straits had overseen the *Under A Red Blood Sky* album. However, once the band were agreed that Eno was the man they most wanted for the job, their persistance amazed everybody. U2 first contacted Eno in the summer of 1983, but he turned them down flat. However, '...they just kept on nagging me, so much so that I listened briefly to some of their old material, which didn't inspire me particularly.' Finally, though, when it became apparent that U2 would not take 'no' for an answer, Eno agreed to meet them. And was immediately hooked.

'Once I'd met Bono I knew I had to work with him. I thought there was something about him, something that made the idea of spending time in a studio with him very interesting. His attitude struck me as very intelligent and inspiring. He talked about how they work as a band, not in terms of playing and so forth, but in terms of contribution, what contributed to the identity of the band as a whole. I hadn't heard anyone talking about a band like that in a long while and so, on that basis, out of curiosity, I agreed to work with them.'

In his own words, Eno went into the studio without any preconceptions and '...therefore had no blindfold to work against. I wasn't acquainted with their work (and) to tell the truth, I was concerned at the outset. I was unsure of what they wanted or expected from me. I emphasised that if I worked with them the record would not sound like anything else they'd done and perhaps that would be a problem.'

It was, in fact, exactly what U2 wanted. They sensed that after three studio albums they were in danger of falling into a simple parody routine, becoming fatally stereotyped as a band who could do nothing more than churn out an endless stream of strident guitar anthems. Just as Eno himself had swerved away from the preconceptions of his 'rock' audience, so U2 wanted to show themselves capable of making music which would display them in an entirely new light. Adam told the New Musical Express' Gavin Martin; '...over the last five years every band in the country has been on the phone to Eno, but we were the only offer he accepted. And the question shouldn't be why we wanted to work with him, but why he wanted to work with us, this pathetic little rock'n'roll band from Dublin who hadn't made a good record since *Boy*. He must have seen something there.'

That something, Bono claimed, was a parallel between the intensity of U2 and the gospel music which had, apparently, been Eno's sole listening matter for three years. 'That was all he had listened to. It was the spirit in which it was made that attracted him to the group's music, the sense of abandonment... (and) I could relate to it. People talk about the spirituality of U2 and I realised that was part of everyday life in black music. I realised that though we weren't rooted in black music, there was something in the spirit that was similar.

'With Eno we rediscovered the spirit in our music and a confidence in ourselves.'

Pride (In The Name Of Love), one of the tracks scheduled for the new album, was released as a single at the beginning of September. it was the band's first single in almost eighteen months and quickly leapt into the top twenty, rubbing shoulders with the endless procession of Wham!, Culture Club and Frankie Goes To Hollywood singles which seemingly had a stranglehold on the imaginations of the record buying public. It was a vibrant song, passionate in the way only U2 could be, effortlessly isolating emotions which few other bands could reach, and draining them. So characteristic was it, that many critics simply laughed off the reports that U2's alliance with Eno was leading them in totally new directions. For them, it was business as usual down at the Windmill Studios.

'I originally wrote *Pride* about Ronald Reagan,' Bono said, 'Reagan and the ambivalent attitude in America. It was originally meant as the sort of pride that won't back down, that wants to build nuclear arsenals. But that wasn't working. I remember a wise old man said to me; "don't try and fight darkness with light, just make the light shine brighter." I was giving Reagan too much importance. Then I thought of Martin Luther King, there's a man. We build the positive rather than fighting with the finger.' The album's closing track, *MLK*, was also inspired by the American civil rights campaigner.

In musical terms, The Edge was to describe *Pride* as; '...the most successful pop song we've ever written. You can see there is a certain craft to the songwriting. I use the word "pop" in the best possible sense; pop for me is an easily understood thing, you listen to it and you comprehend it almost immediately. You relate to it instinctively.

'A lot of the LP isn't like that at all.'

The Unforgettable Fire, U2's fifth album, reached the shops in the first week of October, making its way immediately to number one. That same week, *Under A Blood Red Sky* and *War* were both in the chart as well; at numbers thirty and forty-one respectively. The week before, *October,* too, had been in the top 100 at number ninety-four. In America, the album reached the top ten, six weeks after entering the chart at number forty-seven. The title, *The Unforgettable Fire*, came from the exhibition of paintings which the band had seen at the Chicago Peace Museum; it also related to the drug heroin, something which had destroyed two of Bono's closest friends and which, he claimed, '...informs the LP a lot more than people realise. When your friend becomes a junkie he ceases to be your friend. He'll steal from you, he'll fight you. That had a great effect on me.'

The Edge described *The Unforgettable Fire* as dealing with '...the politics of the individual. We're pulling at areas that we really have strong feelings about; ones we feel we *can* comment on, that relate to our own situation and the situation of our country.

'It's definitely a departure. There's an emphasis away from the guitar, without losing the aggression. I think we were determined to make an LP of contrasts, not just the one dimensional feel, something that had something for everyone. Our audience now is a huge cross section. It's not just fans of *War*— there are people who hated *War* and loved *Boy*, people who hated *Boy* and probably love *Pride*. It's really beginning to widen and I don't feel *War* really showed off the full breadth of our abilities as songwriters or musicians, so that was one of the things that was at the forefront of my mind when we were writing the songs and getting the production together.'

Adam said; 'With this new record we knew we had a very strong base and we could afford taking a few risks, hence Eno coming in. It defined the spirit in which we were going to make the record. It was very much "okay, we'll rehearse the numbers as much as possible, but we're open to basically seeing what happens." This in itself became a problem because we ended up with roughly twenty-five pieces of music and only half the prepared music got on the record. The rest was this stuff we'd created under the influence of Eno.'

One example of this was *Elvis Presley And America*, a song which was recorded in just five minutes. Eno handed Bono a microphone '...and told me to sing over this piece of music which had been slowed down, played backwards, whatever. I said "What? Just like that? Now?" He said "Yes, this is what you're all about." So I did it and when it was finished there were all these beautiful lines and melodies coming out of it. I said I couldn't wait to finish it; Eno said "What do you mean, finish it? It is finished!"'

But Eno was fast to discount accusations that he had simply walked into the studio, Svengali-like, and rearranged U2. 'They were ready,' he said. 'They had it planned. I was merely the guide.'

'Brian and Danny Lanois were very quick to catch the fact that something was in the air and make the appropriate move,' The Edge enthused. '*4th Of July* is (an) example of that. Myself and Adam were just messing around; Brian had some treatments set up for a vocal effect and he patched the guitar into them. Got a rough mix going, it sounded really good so he put it on the quarter inch tape machine. So *4th Of July* never went onto a twenty-four track, it just went straight onto stereo tape. So we've taken a section of improvised live work, almost, and it just captured a lovely mood.'

On August 29, U2 set off on the first leg of their World Tour, embracing Australia, New Zealand, Germany, Italy, France, Belgium, Holland, Switzerland, Britain, Eire and finally, the U.S.A. Six weeks previous, Bono alone appeared onstage with Bob Dylan at the visiting American's gig at Slane Castle. U2 had been invited to perform at the show, but declined; it wasn't right for them, they claimed. Bono took the stage for the encore, improvising a version of Dylan's protest classic *Blowin' In The Wind*, much to the outrage of the audience, but to the delight of Dylan. His own children, he confided, are U2 fans. Dylan and Bono also found time to exchange a few words by way of an interview which was later published in Hot Press.

The tour was not without its memorable moments. In Sydney, Australia; 'We came out and started playing *Gloria* in two different keys. Adam came onstage and because he's tone deaf he didn't even notice!' In Paris, the venue was a large tent set in the decaying industrial heartlands where the movie *Diva* was filmed; in Brussels, the band's amplification set off an earthquake alarm at the nearby Belgium Royal Observatory. The Edge blamed it on Adam's bass pedals.

The British dates opened with two nights at the Brixton Academy, fast establishing itself as one of the most important venues in London, before moving on to gigs in Glasgow, Edinburgh, Birmingham and Manchester. The show then returned to London, for two nights at the massive Wembley Arena.

From there the band's itinerary took them to Ireland and, after that, the United States for a handful of pre-Christmas shows as a prelude for a more extensive visit early in 1985. There was not much room for any free time in the schedule, but, faced with a one day break on November 25, Bono and Alan returned to London from Dublin to pledge their support to the Band Aid project. The Edge had also been invited to participate; unfortunately at the last minute he was taken ill.

This had been put together by fellow Dubliner Bob Geldof, and Midge Ure of Ultravox, a project designed to bring together some, if not all, of the top stars of the day to raise money for the victims of the Ethiopian famine. (According to Geldof, just three of the people he invited along considered themselves 'too important to give up a Sunday morning to save another human being'). This vast array of talent, dubbed 'The Greatest Rock Group In The World' by the Daily Mirror, pooled their resources for just two songs; a Geldof/Ure composition called *Do They Know It's Christmas?* and *Feed The World,* which featured the *...Christmas* backing track overdubbed with Christmas messages from some of the participants. The session was filmed by seven television crews and shown

on nationwide TV before appearing as a video, given headline coverage by most of the popular tabloid papers and the results, predictably, rocketed straight to number one in the chart. Over 600,000 copies were sold during the first five days after the single's release; total sales of over three million were confidently predicted by all concerned, even by those like Wham's George Michael whose own product was in direct competition with Band Aid. The single did indeed fulfil all such predictions. It stayed at number one through-out the Christmas period (only to be dislodged by Foreigner, of all people) and made the top ten in America. The corresponding video also topped the chart.

Bono took one of the lead vocal lines and Bob Geldof, in an interview with Melody Maker's Barry McIlhenney, recalled; 'It was really funny, James Taylor out of Kool And The Gang arrives, you know, THE voice, and suddenly no one wants to sing in front of him! Like Bono and (Paul) Weller are really freaking out at having to sing with this guy there, it was that sort of mutual respect atmosphere.'

The euphoria of the Band Aid single carried on well into 1985, culminating in the Live Aid concerts, staged simultaneously in London and Philadelphia on July 13. U2's set, at the time, seemed just another heartbeat to save in the memory banks for analysis when the madness was finally over; when that time came it was evident they had done themselves proud. They had time for just two songs: *Sunday Bloody Sunday*, of course, was the one we all expected to hear, but *Bad* stayed in our minds the longest, pulsating, almost punishing, possibly the highlight of the entire afternoon. Certainly when Bono left the stage, and reached into the crowd to find someone to dance with, the spontaneity of the simple gesture touched everyone who saw it.

For U2, the seven months leading up to Live Aid were spent, for the most part, on the road. In April they headlined New York's Madison Square Garden for the first time, the 20,000 available tickets disappearing within one hour of going on sale; in June they appeared at Dublin's Croke Park as the highlight of a week long festival in the city, and in between times they turned up at the Milton Keynes Bowl for a show whose reception alone was enough to drown out the midsummer rain which turned the entire site into a quagmire.

"Even in the miserable drizzle U2 were so hot I was gulping down malaria tablets," wrote Gary Bushell in Sounds. "Such power, such passion, such glorious intensity." Other people remarked on the sheer *diversity* of the audience the band were attracting; the other acts on the bill that afternoon – R.E.M., Spear Of Destiny, Billy Bragg – had something to do with that, but it wasn't an isolated phenomenon. The Edge said, "We seem to have reinvented the touring strategy for breaking a band, which no-one else did for a long time. Our album sales have never reflected our live business. We don't sell as many as you might expect. The diversity you see at our shows is purely that these people have heard about the shows through their friends. I'm sure a lot of them don't buy U2 records – well they don't, or we'd sell a lot more albums.

"At the same time, what we're doing must have some sort of universal appeal, it's not a hybrid thing. It's not designed for people who know all about the Velvet Underground. I think a lot of groups need that context, but there are people who wouldn't know Lou Reed if they met him on the street. Most of it is down to Bono, because he has the ability to communicate in a way that most people, be they Italian, Dutch, German or American, can understand, and that's remarkable."

Live Aid was in many ways the end result of that ability to communicate. Other bands were invited to appear because they were famous, because they were successful, because they were there. But U2 would have

been on the bill even if they were still simply packing 'em in at the pub down the road. That they had advanced way, way further than that was immaterial, although few people would argue when Bono said, "Isn't it odd . . . we're playing better than ever in these places that we ran away from for so long. I remember our first gig in America, at the Mudd Club in New York and these people from Premier Talent coming up to us and saying, 'It's gonna be interesting when you play Madison Square Garden.'

"I mean, that was everything we were against, and we were against playing these aircraft hangars right up until the time I went to see Bruce Springsteen at Wembley Arena. Now I enjoy playing these places – instead of a backdrop of stained glass windows we've got people. And we are making big music. When we start *Pride*, that *floats* over the audience, and to confine it is living a lie.

"But we're the antithesis of those big rock 'n' roll bands. This is not the cycle complete again, this is a garageband that has left garageland, because we are the first of that generation of bands. Not The Clash and Sex Pistols generation, but the generation that was in their audience."

Shortly after the release of *The Unforgettable Fire*, discussing the break of almost two years which separated that album from *War*, Bono joked, "We broke up the band. We literally broke up the band, and formed another band with the same name and the same members. That's what we did. Then we had all those teething problems that you have when you start a new band." U2 took another break following Live Aid, but this time the silence did not seem quite so impenetrable. A new single, the title track from *The Unforgettable Fire,* was the first of several releases to leak into the shops over the next few months, records which, even with the hefty import tag which accompanied the likes of *Wide Awake In America,* kept the band's name alive.

Bono, too, was to prove irrepressible. Several years previous, in November 1982, he said, "I was out in my car, and the first time I heard *Theme From Harry's Game* . . . it suddenly came on and I nearly came right off the road and crashed! I thought it was the end of the world and I was in Heaven!" He was talking about a single by another Irish group, Clannad. Some half dozen albums old at that point, Clannad inhabited a magical land somewhere between tradition and pop; in their earliest days their live set varied between Irish folk and Gaelic translations of The Beach Boys' greatest hits, a combination which won them a regional talent contest and a major recording deal very early on in their career. They turned it down, but by 1979 this one-family group – singer Maire Ni Bhraonain, Ciaran and Pol 0 Braonain are sister and brothers, Padgraig and Noel O Dugain their uncles – was recording for the Irish Gael-Linn label. *Theme From Harry's Game* gave Clannad a totally unexpected top five hit; now they were preparing to release a track from their ninth album, *Macalla*, as a single – and straight away the rock press sat up and took notice. Guesting on lead vocals, singing alongside Maire, was Bono.

"There's always been a lot of mutual respect between us and Bono," said Maire. "It's great that a band from Ireland can get as high as they have done. I threw in Bono's name as a suggestion because it connected better with the songs we were thinking of doing." She continued, "We had already decided that we wouldn't release the song unless it was *great.* If it was merely *good* we wouldn't have gone ahead. Bono came into the studio and we talked about it and he seemed to feel good about the song once he had heard it. But I've never seen anyone just go into a song like that."

According to legend, Bono sat through one playback of *In A Lifetime,* asked to hear it again and then simply burst into song. "He sang what he felt," Maire said, "Words and melody. It sounds like a fairy tale, but it's true. It just seemed to happen in the best possible way."

Bono added, "This group Clannad are very real, but they are also very unique. Sometimes you wonder if they really exist because they are so unique as a family. But there's nothing real about them. The only thing that's weird about them is that they're so unreal.

"I wouldn't want people to see this as U2 doing something with Clannad. Clannad, as a group, were once associated purely with Irish folk and now they are moving towards a jazzy area. It's becoming quite a hybrid really."

Adam told the New Musical Express: "There's an intelligence in Clannad's music, but there's also a soul. It's not something you can fake. It's just something that's there, something in the quality of their life."

In A Lifetime eventually made it into the top 20, a surprisingly poor showing but one which passed most U2-watchers by as the action moved swiftly to another stage. Throughout their most recent American tour, U2 were seen to be concerning themselves more and more with the burgeoning Human Rights movement, and in particular its attempts to remedy the situation in South Africa – *Pride* was regularly preluded by some reference to the anti-apartheid struggle, while the band's efforts were recognised – with a phone call shortly before the band took the stage – from the South African black church leader Desmond Tutu. According to NME's Adrian Thrills, however, Bono played down "his potential political impact."

"I'm just like anyone else," Bono told him. "I watch the television and read the papers and I don't really know what's going on, especially regarding something like South Africa. I'm just as numb and mummified as anyone else." However, he continued, "I use my songs as a way to awaken myself. It's like sticking a needle in your leg after it has gone to sleep." In January, one such song appeared on the Artists United Against Apartheid album, *Sun City.* It was immediately acclaimed the most important song on the entire set.

Bono had already pledged his support to the project long before he recorded *Silver And Gold* with Keith Richard and Ronnie Wood. He appeared on both the album's title track and in the accompanying video, and it was whilst he was in New York for the shooting of the film that he ran into the two Rolling Stones. When Bono asked if they would be interested in joining him in the studio to record this one song, the pair jumped at the chance. Forty-eight hours later *Silver And Gold* was completed, and the album's producers, Steve Van Zandt and Arthur Baker, delayed mastering the rest of the album while they mixed Bono's last minute contribution.

"It's the first song that I've ever written that comes from somebody else's point of view," Bono said. "U2 songs are always from my own point of view, but this is a departure into the third person. It's also the first blues-influenced song that I've written. I play my guitar with my foot miked up, the way that old bluesmen like Robert Johnson do. And I'm banging the sides of my guitar with my knuckles to keep the rhythm. As the song goes on the tempo keeps getting faster and the mood more and more intense."

In November, 1985, *The Unforgettable Fire* logged its 100th week in the chart, giving U2 membership of that exclusive club formed by bands who had achieved a similar century with three consecutive albums: The Beatles, Simon & Garfunkel and Dire Straits were the only other members. Such a statistic could not help but remind people it was time U2 unleashed their next record breaker, and as the new year loomed the word from Windmill Lane was that that time was fast approaching. And in March it arrived, with the release of *The Joshua Tree*.

Once again, production chores were handled by Brian Eno and Daniel Lanois, Eno presumably still referring to "Rock 'n' Roll" with the same crafty wink he had given Bono the first time he mentioned the subject. Like its predecessor, *The Joshua Tree* offered the veteran U2 fan few points of immediate reference, although the crisp Steve Lillywhite remix which graced four of the tracks — the singles *Where The Streets Have No Name* and *With Or Without You, Bullet The Blue Sky* and *Red Hill Mining Town* — did much to startle the listener out of the mood which the remaining tracks so painstakingly created. *Bullet The Blue Sky* in particular came searing off the vinyl, a mesmeric bass heavy number which reflected nothing so much as the sound of The Stooges or the Velvet Underground, updated and refined for the requirements of an audience weaned on the sophistication of Eighties' stadium rock.

The Joshua Tree clung once again to the visions of America which *The Unforgettable Fire* had spawned, a feeling which was reinforced by the videos which accompanied the singles from the album — a rooftop performance in Los Angeles, an impromptu miming session on the streets of Las Vegas. There was a ragged innocence to those images, one which hinted at the various interpretations of the songs which one could make, but which neither expected nor demanded any more involvement from the watcher than that.

Neither did the music itself offer any of those portentous statements for which U2 have so often been criticised. There was a generous ambiguity to Eno's production, and while an underlying harshness indicated that not even his influence could ever draw U2 totally away from the music which had pushed them into contention in the first place, still it was the sentiments which the lyrics conjured up which demonstrated where U2's heart truly was.

The Edge told Melody Maker's Colin Irwin: "Bono's writing words in a way he hasn't done up until now. He's so much better a singer, and we're listening to different things now. We're getting more interested in the classical songwriters . . . country singers and stuff. It's like we really didn't discover our Irishness until we travel-

led out of Ireland, and then you go to America and find yourself completely alienated by it. Then slowly, you realise there are different levels to it. The America of the great R&B and country performers, and in civil rights people like Martin Luther King and Bobby Kennedy. We worked with T-Bone Burnett and Robbie Robertson and Bono did a session with Keith Richard, people who are hooked up on that. And some of the writers, the new journalism of people like Truman Capote and Norman Mailer . . . the way they were able to bring you to a place [was] almost cinematic. We tried to do that on the album."

Later Larry said: "We wanted to try and capture a place as well as a mood, we wanted to give each song a sense of location. That's something that Eno is very good at, getting into the ideas behind a song. Most producers are less inclined to get involved in that side of things. They're keener on simply getting the record to sound right." Thus the album's final track, *Mothers Of The Disappeared*, echoed all Bono saw — and heard — when he visited El Salvador and Nicaragua shortly before work began on the LP. "I was drawn towards central America after meeting Rene Castro (the Chilean painter rescued from imprisonment by Amnesty International, with whom Bono also toured America during 1986). At first he didn't pay me much attention until he discovered the Amnesty connection. People from the Latin American community came to our gigs and Rene Castro sent me some of his paintings, and eventually I was asked to go to Nicaragua and El Salvador . . . "

The situation in Nicaragua he described as "the sexiest revolution I ever saw". Salvador affected him more deeply. "You could feel the atmosphere of malevolence coming from the troops. It was awful. I wrote *Bullet The Blue Sky* out of the fear I felt there, using very primitive imagery. Because Salvador looks like an ordinary city . . . "

The album as a whole was dedicated to Greg Carroll, a Maori whom U2 employed during the *Unforgettable Fire* tour. "He was almost flesh and blood with U2," said Bono. "We met him in Auckland, New Zealand. Auckland is a city set around five volcanic mounds and the smallest one is called One Tree Hill because there's a tree at the top of it. He was one of those guys you say he's too good for this world. We haven't, and I don't think we ever will, get over his loss. And he

died doing me a favour (he was delivering Bono's motorcycle to him; on the way back he crashed and was killed). He further made 1986 a paradoxical year in our lives. That's why the desert attracted me as an image. That year was really a desert for us. It was a terrible time." The song, *One Tree Hill*, was Bono's own personal tribute to Greg.

"I think this record, more than any of the others, says what we want to say. Certainly for me, as the word writer in the band. In a way it doesn't need me . . . to explain it. After a while it does sink in, the way it's put together from beginning to end. The significance of the name *The Joshua Tree* – it's almost impossible for me to explain that seriously, for me to take myself as seriously as that. There are many reasons for it . . . inevitably we're going to lie a lot!" (The Joshua Tree is actually a rare species of yucca plant, believed by the American Indians to possess magical powers. Gram Parsons, the country-rock singer whose influence has seemingly touched every "sensitive" songwriter to emerge in the past decade, asked that when he died he should

be cremated at the Joshua Tree National Monument – a request which was duly – if illegally – carried out by Parsons' road manager, Phil Kaufman, following the singer's death, in 1973).

"Rock 'n' Roll is caught up in adolescence," said Bono. "It has failed to cross into real relationships, the violence of love and sexuality is ignored, and I'm interested in going into that. And that's what U2 can contribute – there's an odd mixture of love and anger in the group."

The album's reception left little to be desired. While some critics viewed it with caution, their words plainly chosen with care as they pondered whether to applaud U2 maintaining the direction of *The Unforgettable Fire* or lament their failure to step even further into the unknown, the public responded with immediate delight. Straight into the U.K. album chart at number one, in America *The Joshua Tree* took only three weeks to emulate it, clinging then to the top spot with leech-like tenacity. It remained there for the best part of three months, and three months after that was still in the Top Ten.

Singles from the album, too, pushed U2 into the highest echelons, and that despite such reservations as The Edge evinced when questioned about the band's past Top 30 record. "The last time we were on Top Of The Pops, we were the first group that went on and our record went *down!*" That was *Pride*, and its ultimate placing of number three was "the highest chart placing we've ever had, but we're really terrible at producing singles. We're never prepared to work out all that remix stuff and all those other promotional devices, it's never been a priority with us." Now the group found themselves virtually taking up residence in the British top five with a triumvirate of singles beginning with *With Or Without You* in March, continuing through the sublime magnificence of *I Still Haven't Found What I'm Looking For* and on to the album's opening cut, *Where The Streets Have No Name,* which was flirting with the top five *six* months after the release of the album itself.

U2 themselves celebrated the release of *The Joshua Tree* by launching themselves onto another characteristically massive world tour, kicking off in the United States where performances of *MLK, Pride* and *Bullet . . .* prompted the English Sounds to describe them as " . . . almost unimpeachable . . . as radical as a rock band can be". From there they made their way homewards, headlining two shows at Wembley and a handful more around the United Kingdom en route for a triumphant Irish homecoming in August. And throughout, they were truly able to show off all they had learned since their last time out, calmly assimilating old and new into a set which, although it left a few veteran diehards suddenly wondering where the rest of the good old days had gone, showed U2 to be considerably more aware of their own great traditions than their critics, at least, gave them credit for.

This was no tired supergroup going through the motions for the umpteenth time in as many evenings, even from the back of the largest stadium the band *communicated*. On the night it didn't even matter that *Sunday Bloody Sunday*, a condemnation of mob ignorance suddenly became a celebration of it, a terrace chant rabble rouser which Sounds' Roy Wilkinson believed "should have long since been abandoned" for that reason. Like a club band playing the sweatiest dive, U2 were able to reach the furthest recesses of the hall and at the end of the evening, even the skies overhanging Wembley Stadium were sweating.

A decade ago, when U2 first came together to play whichever venue would let them, that was always what they were best at. Today they've still got it down pat, and if ever the age-old cliché, "Success hasn't changed them" needed personification, you'd have to look a long way to find anyone better qualified than U2. "Lou Reed recently did an interview where he talked about U2 and he said we were at odds with everything that was going on," Bono said. "In our organisation, our road crew, our attitude to money, it was all something different." That, perhaps, sums U2 up better than anything. They really are something different.

DISCOGRAPHY

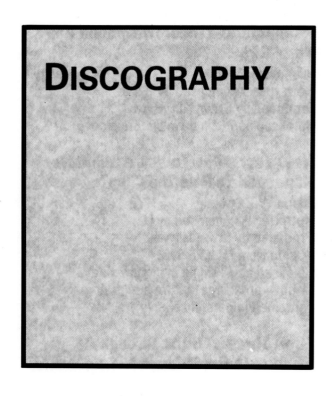

SINGLES

U2 – 3 (EP) Out Of Control/Stories For Boys/ Boy-Girl
(December 1979, Eire only)

Another Day/Twilight
(February 1980, Eire only)

11 O'Clock Tick Tock/Touch
(May 1980)

A Day Without Me/Things To Make And Do
(August 1980)

I Will Follow/Boy-Girl (live)
(October 1980)

Fire/J Swallo
(July 1981)
(Also double 7" with Cry/The Electric Co./ 11 O'Clock Tick Tock/The Ocean)

Gloria/I Will Follow (live)
(September 1981)

A Celebration/Trash, Trampoline & The Party Girl
(March 1982)

New Year's Day/Treasure (Whatever Happened To Pete The Chop?)
(January 1983)
(Also double 7" and 12" with Fire/I Threw A Brick/A Day Without Me)

Two Hearts Beat As One/Endless Deep
(March 1983)
(Also double 7" New Year's Day and US mixes)

Pride (In The Name Of Love)/Boomerang II
(September 1984)
(Also double 7" and 12" with 4th Of July/ Boomerang I)

The Unforgettable Fire/A Sort Of Homecoming (live)
(May 1985)
(Also double 7" with The Three Sunrises/Love Comes Tumbling/Sixty Seconds in Kingdom Come; 12" also with Bass Trap)

With Or Without You/Luminous Times (Hold On To Love)
(March 1987)
(Also 12" with Walk To The Water)

I Still Haven't Found What I'm Looking For/ Spanish Eyes/Deep In The Heart
(May 1987)

Where The Streets Have No Name/Race Against Time
(August 1987)
(Also 12" with Silver And Gold/Sweetest Thing)

ALBUMS

BOY
I Will Follow/Twilight/An Cat Dubh/Into The Heart/Out Of Control/Stories For Boys/The Ocean/A Day Without Me/Another Time, Another Place/The Electric Co./Shadows And Tall Trees.
(November 1980)

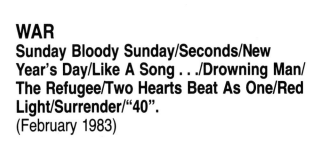

OCTOBER
Gloria/I Fall Down/I Threw A Brick/Rejoice/ Fire/Tomorrow/October/With A Shout/ Stranger In A Strange Land/Scarlet/Is That All?
(November 1981)

WAR
Sunday Bloody Sunday/Seconds/New Year's Day/Like A Song . . ./Drowning Man/ The Refugee/Two Hearts Beat As One/Red Light/Surrender/"40".
(February 1983)

UNDER A BLOOD RED SKY
**Gloria/11 O'Clock Tick Tock/I Will Follow/
Party Girl/Sunday Bloody Sunday/The
Electric Co./New Year's Day/"40".**
(November 1983)

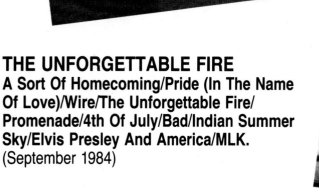

THE UNFORGETTABLE FIRE
**A Sort Of Homecoming/Pride (In The Name
Of Love)/Wire/The Unforgettable Fire/
Promenade/4th Of July/Bad/Indian Summer
Sky/Elvis Presley And America/MLK.**
(September 1984)

WIDE AWAKE IN AMERICA
**Bad (live)/A Sort Of Homecoming (live)/
Three Sunrises/A Love Comes Tumbling.**
(May 1985 – USA only but imported in mass
quantities)

THE JOSHUA TREE
**Where The Streets Have No Name/I Still
Haven't Found What I'm Looking For/With Or
Without You/Bullet The Blue Sky/Running To
Stand Still/Red Hill Mining Town/In God's
Country/Trip Through Your Wires/One Tree
Hill/Exit/Mothers Of The Disappeared.**
(March 1987)